Modern Artists

Chryssa

Harry N. Abrams, Inc., Publishers, New York

Sam Hunter

Chryssa

Series Editor: Werner Spies

Library of Congress Cataloging in Publication Data

Hunter, Sam, 1923–
   Chryssa.

   1. Chryssa, Varda, 1933–
NB237.C48H86   730'.92'4   74–6199
ISBN 0-8108-4409-X

Library of Congress Catalogue Card Number: 74–6199
Harry N. Abrams, Incorporated, New York
Copyright 1974 in Germany by Verlag Gerd Hatje, Stuttgart
Printed and bound in West Germany

The artist Chryssa is a dark, handsome, and mercurial woman so dominated by her sense of artistic mission, to the exclusion of all other considerations, that it becomes difficult for an observer to reconcile her theatrical personal style with the cool, controlled objectivism and technical precision of the exquisite light boxes on which her artistic reputation rests. Everything about her carefully constructed neon sculptures testifies to esthetic sobriety, finesse and a fanatical patience. Yet she is known as an artist who can make strong workmen and artisan assistants blanch by her eruptions of cold fury, especially when some fabricated sculpture element she ordered does not meet her exact specifications. She demands in others the same perfectionism she has come to expect of herself. With less provocation, she frets and fumes at the frustrations of urban life in New York, and often overreacts to the petty rivalries, real or imagined slights and the internal politics of the art world. Since 1961 she has had a number of New York dealers representing her work, and all of them were exceptional in taste and intelligence, and generally effective promoters of vanguard art. Yet she has restlessly, almost compulsively, changed dealer representatives on rather flimsy pretexts whenever she sensed that their commitment to her work was less than total. As a result of her occasional temperamental indulgences and moodiness, apocrypha and legend seem to collect around her name.

Yet, while Chryssa is clearly hyper-sensitive to criticism, and strong-willed, her reputation as an *enfant terrible* is quite undeserved. Her personality, indeed, can best be understood against the background of her European origins and culture. An ingrained ambivalence about American life and mores is compounded equally of ecstatic affirmations and mistrust. Essentially mediterranean in her simplicity of outlook, she finds the headlong pace and anonymity of American life still somewhat unsettling after nearly twenty years of residence.

She was raised and educated in Athens, left Greece to study art in Paris in 1953, and then came to live first in San Francisco, and then in New York two years later. The bustling energy of this city, the highly visible drama of popular culture played out in public places, especially in the spectacle of commercial signs, combined with the new eloquence of emerging American art in the fifties to directly form her own sculpture, which is unmistakably a cultural product of the New York experience. Nonetheless, Chryssa has never been able satisfactorily to identify with American existence as a whole, and the pastoral landscape of her youth always seems to beckon like the dream of some departed golden age. She maintains her traditional, European affiliations and manages to restore her spirit and equanimity by making frequent trips abroad. The occasion may be professional, or simply pleasurable, and most often it is a combination of the two.

In 1969, she painted six thirteen-foot-high canvases for Count Peter Metternich, whom she had met the previous summer of 1968 at the international *Documenta* exhibition in Kassel, Germany. This was her first painting commission, providing her with a unique opportunity to create a whole visual environment for the great salon and dining hall of the ancestral family *Schloss* in Adelebsen. It was a treasured and typical gambit; she was delighted to escape the discommoding New York art world, in dead of winter, as it happened, and 'to meet all available royalty' in the Metternich circle. Beyond the element of mild snobbism, it was gratifying to produce an ambitious project for a titled European family who were as attentive to her personal needs as they were socially appealing. Many

American artists actually prefer not to meet their collectors, because they may be overly demanding, intellectually flat, or otherwise

tiresome. Today, with radical changes in the very nature of art, which has grown to monstrously outsize landscape objects, or vanished into vast conceptual projects, questions have been raised about the feasibility of owning or displaying works of art at all, either privately or publicly. Chryssa, however, seems still to thrive and depend upon the classical artist-patron relationship, a situation which the competitive scramble of the New York art world does very little to encourage. Her European education and orientation towards situations of protective patronage make the factionalism, professional uncertainties and instant history-making of the New York art world appear even more appalling and distracting than they actually are. For these and other reasons, she stands apart from the art 'scene' and maintains a certain reserve, and even suspicion of it. This defensive pose unfortunately tends to obscure her natural warmth, gregariousness and considerable wit. One could not guess, from her grave mien and guarded manner on public occasions, that she is a gifted raconteur and mimic capable of stripping the self-important characters in her professional circle—eminent artists, museum officials, influential collectors—of their pretensions. It is this hidden, playful side of her personality which makes her such an intense delight to her friends with whom she relaxes from the tensions of work.

When Chryssa began her pioneering experiments in the new mode of 'luminist' sculpture early in this decade, she found herself laboring under the double penalty of breaking ground in unfamiliar esthetic territory, and directly challenging the sacrosanct technical procedures of a variety of conservative but indispensable artisans, electricians, glass blowers and shop managers not in the habit of responding to fresh initiatives from outsiders. Unlike some of the minimalist sculptors today, she is not able to proceed on the assumption that her designs will be fabricated into a satisfactory artifact by anonymous workmen, without her attentive and continuous intervention. Her eye and touch are required at every stage of the creative process to assure the requisite intricacy of structure or circuitry, and appropriate levels of color and light intensity. While her neon sculpture distills something of the visual delirium and throbbing urgencies of nocturnal Times Square, within a highly refined and transforming artistic idiom, the message is by no means simple, or necessarily compatible with elementary commercial signs whose style and forms have been appropriated. The commercial sources of her work provide a facade masking a complex artistic order, and a decision-making process over which the artist, given her natural inclinations, agonizes from the moment of conception to finished execution. The coherence and clarity of the end product is a measure of her profound knowledge of, and total immersion in, the technological process.

Chryssa began producing accomplished work at the astonishing age of twenty-two, and she has remained a significant and consistently innovative figure in the art world ever since. After a brief study period in Paris and a short-lived residence in San Francisco, she came to live in New York, and it was here in 1955 that her first distinctly personal work emerged in her so-called *Cycladic Books* (page 25). These undetailed, virtually featureless reliefs in clay were marked only by vertical and horizontal divisions, forming a wide T. The tablets ambiguously recalled the vague, flattened masks of Cycladic sculpture (the horizontal ridges could be read as eye sockets, and the vertical depression as nose), but they also anticipated the forms of reductive, hard-edge painting of the late fifties, although a precedent for such austere inventions already existed in the paintings of Rothko, Newman and Reinhardt. Admittedly these were unlikely and esoteric sources for contemporary sculpture, and Chryssa actually stood quite alone in her interests and strikingly original plastic formulations at the time. The softly creased reliefs also offered the first evidence of what was to become a dominating obsession on her part with the problems both of visibility and legibility in art. It is interesting to note in this regard that Chryssa herself brings up the name of the painter Agnes Martin as one of the first New York artists whom she knew and respected. The faint intelligibility of Martin's repeated markings and formalized *graffiti* do have a bearing on her own forms and content. Chryssa's 'empty' *Cycladic Books* may also be seen as a prediction in terms of flat relief, much closer in spirit to painting than sculpture, of the Minimalist rage which followed in the sixties.

The next year Chryssa created a group of shallow boxes with hinged glass covers containing rows of immovable plaster letters. One such ensemble (1956; page 28) spelled out the word BACH in a rather mystifying way. Three horizontal tiers of repeated letter clusters were inserted sideways, at right angles to the frontal plane, so that the exposed edges became an unreadable, abstract map of linear accents. But a key to the puzzle was provided in a legible sequence of letters at the bottom of the structure. This was the kind of conundrum and artfully planned visual confusion which Jasper Johns was just then making the basis of a virtual revolution in art. Although Rauschenberg had already incorporated large stencilled letters and word fragments in his paintings by 1956, no one ventured to explore the potential of words as the exclusive content of painting or sculpture. Johns' 'Flags', 'Targets' and 'Numbers' series were not exhibited publicly until 1958 and 1960, by which time an historic shift in sensibility away from Action painting towards either a more object-oriented or a conceptual art had already begun. The closed and complete letter systems which Chryssa so meticulously elaborated were, so far as one can determine, entirely unprecedented, and they thus deserve the highest priorities as a significant contributing factor in the important new developments then taking place.

Typographic, symmetrized compositions of metal forms in shallow relief, based on impressions of newsprint, whole newspaper pages and moulds, and then vast enlargements in raised relief of single letters made up of many small, uniform components, followed in her art. For sculpture, these experimental ventures represented a ground-breaking effort and did seem to parallel Johns' investigation of a new artistic order of regularized form and objective meanings taken from visual commonplaces. The two artists shared an almost programmatic reaction to the exhausted visual rhetoric and ego-centered expressionism of the Action painters. In their separate and distinct ways, they both turned to banal and popular image sources at precisely the same artistic moment. Chryssa's precocious use of repeated, multiple imagery of pop culture origin, first in her series *Tablets* and *Plaques* (pages 26 and 27), and then in the *Newspapers* (pages 44/49) and *Projections*, between the years 1956 and 1961, was revealed dramatically at the Guggenheim Museum in a significant retrospective show of 1961. In retrospect, the small exhibition now seems most prophetic and highly original. In an introduction to a gallery show catalogue some time later, the critic Diane Waldman noted that, 'Although Moholy-Nagy and Thomas Wilfred were pioneers in the use of light, the first major event in its recent history occurred with Pop'. Of course, the assimilation of mass media imagery and their techniques of presentation, as a new form of the *objet trouvé*, had appeared prior to official Pop Art in the work of

Rauschenberg and Johns. It was this interest in pictorial cliches, commercial signs, lettrist sources, and flat 'fields' of repeated, fractured words which logically drew Chryssa to pop culture as her inspiration even before she ventured into light art. Her newspaper subjects, such as the monumental, exquisitely painted *Magic Carpet* (1962, pages 48/49), with its ten-foot spread of duplicated rubber stamps taken from the actual press plates of the *New York Times* classified section, in 1962, actually anticipated the uniform, multiple imagery of postage stamps or Coca-Cola bottles which Andy Warhol later showed publicly. Other examples by Chryssa of banal illustration include her *Automobile Tires* (page 34) and *Cigarette Lighter* (page 35), which she has dated 1959—62. These paintings employ effects roughly comparable to the silkscreening of commercial imagery on canvas that was later widely adapted after the example first of Warhol and then of Rauschenberg.

Interestingly enough, at the same time that Chryssa was creating a kind of microscopic cosmos of uniform 'all-over' detail in her large stamped canvases, she also found herself moving in the opposite direction of isolating holistic, individual letters, such as her *Letter E* (1957—60, page 31) and *Letter H* (1957—60, pages 32 and 33), and magnifying them to heroic scale. These single or unitary images created an essentially abstract icon in an orginal type of sculptural relief. The studies of various letters, particularly the *Letter E*, coincided in time with her *Arrow Homage to Times Square* (1957, page 30), a work which clearly indicates that the interplay of light and cast shadow on a raised surface already engaged the artist's attention. Her quintessential subject matter of light play, stemming from the visual dynamics of Times Square, are thus already prefigured by this early work and its title. Given the irresistible logic of her artistic growth, and her responsiveness to milieu, both artistic and social, it required only a short step to progress from the raised tablets and plaster reliefs of monumental individual letters with their shadow play, to her more direct 'homages' in neon to Times Square, a locale which has always epitomized for her America's raw power and vitality. Chryssa later summarized her feelings on this score in an interview of 1968 in *Women's Wear Daily:* 'America is very stimulating, intoxicating for me. Believe me when I say that there is wisdom, indeed, in the flashing lights of Times Square. The vulgarity of America as seen in the lights of Times Square is poetic, extremely poetic. A foreigner can observe this, describe this. Americans feel it.'

Recalling those first exciting New York years with nostalgia, Chryssa remembers herself as 'utterly alone, broke and very happy', a solitary seeker after novel artistic meanings who haunted the anonymous streets as well as the museums and galleries of the city, and was already magnetized by the visual spectacle of popular culture. With her Greek background, she still tends to look for classical references everywhere in contemporary experience. 'I was naturally drawn to Times Square', she reminisces. 'Times Square I knew had this great wisdom—it was Homeric—even if the sign-makers did not realize that.' In the inexhaustible fantasy and nocturnal blaze of New York's most enthralling 'light show' Chryssa thus discovered her basic inspiration. The 'spiralic' form and 'flat linear approach' of the commercial neon sign-makers made contact across the ages, she now believes and avers, with her Byzantine heritage and an interest in El Greco's serpentine flicker. Whether or not she conceived of 'low', or publicly available art in such exalted terms and with such reverence at the time, she did embark boldly on a new series of compositions using 'junk' signs and metal word fragments in 1959. 1(

By 1962, a pioneering work entitled *Times Square Sky* (page 42) introduced a delicate thread of neon script spelling the word 'air', as a kind of grace note within a scrambled assemblage of fractured metal letters. The illuminated word was not merely inventive flourish or a self-conscious *tour de force*. It became a source of deep personal liberation and, finally, represented nothing less than an influential advance in content and manner for American art. The next year Chryssa committed herself more decisively to neon and light works with one of her most important and ambitious compositions, which she called *Americanoom*. Here, an even larger, more emphatic panel of neon letters created a strong visual counterpoint against an identical band of word fragments in metal, as if to demonstrate that solid, material metal and insubstantial form possessed equal artistic prerogatives, and were in fact alternating aspects of each other. It took only another short step to compose in neon tubing exclusively. With great originality and powerful conviction, Chryssa thus managed to give definition and structure to the least nameable of substances, hitherto considered inaccessible to art: colored light and air.

'Light Art', so called, was only just beginning to make its way internationally. Yves Klein, the French neo-dada best known for pressing nude girls smeared with pigment on blank canvases, had created a blue light 'environment' in the late fifties. That gesture represented just one skirmish in a broad campaign to desanctify the material art object as such, and to soak the world and atmosphere in I.K.B.—initials which stood for the exuberant shade of blue of Klein's monochrome paintings, and his designated trademark which he liked to call International Klein Blue. Shortly after, three young German vanguard artists banded together in the 'Group Zero' (they included Klein's brother-in-law, Günther Uecker), and created a loose kind of outdoor light 'happening' with powerful projectors, aluminum foil, soap bubbles, white balloons and the mobile forms of the spectators themselves. Thomas Wilfred's 'Clavilux', a color organ, had long been a mild source of curiosity at the Museum of Modern Art, producing bland, euphoric 'light ballets' and streaming color compositions which did, however, anticipate in a much lower key the eye-rocking, mind-blowing light shows of the psychedelic sixties. Even more authoritative precedents for electrified art existed, such as Moholy-Nagy's light-machine of his German Bauhaus period. However, it finally took a unique combination of Pop Art, McLuhanism and the new cult of technology in the sixties (a cult which included the technology of the human eye and retinal dynamics, in the form of 'Op Art') to create an unprecedented, effective climate for successful experiment in a variety of light media, and intermedia. Historically, Chryssa was actually the first artist to use direct emitted electric light and neon (rather than projected or screened light). Her imagery was also unique, since its source was the lettered commercial signs of the urban environment rather than art history or past styles of expression.

Her early light box series contained neon variations on the letters W, A and the ampersand, aligned in refulgent, parallel banks. The repeating effect of the letters produced sensations of resonating light impulses, rather like expanding and contracting ripples in a visible fluid medium, even though there was no actual movement. The kinetic effect was all induced in the eye of the observer. Mounted in handsome, dark Plexiglas boxes, the curving neon tubes, their electrical connections and interior working parts were clearly exposed to view. These transparent cubes of light thus became not only visually potent but psychologically involving, for they could be apprehended both as finished form and works-in-progress. The glamorous illusion of electrified neon, and the visible technology of circuitry enhanced each other's impact, and together supported the statement of revealed artistic process which these novel inventions embodied. Soon after, Chryssa began to program her light boxes to go on and off, with uncomfortably long waiting periods between light phase and dark. The timed lapses of light added a new dimension of strain to the game of illusionism, and the work of art now offered itself to the spectator as both presence and absence, a direct and subliminal experience.

Clarifying her objectives in succeeding exhibitions, Chryssa permitted the neon tubing to escape its containers, to which were now consigned only the electrical mechanism, often densely elaborate in structure. It was a nice point whether the internal circuitry or the extruded tubing had become the more essential sculptural experience, but there was in any event a more direct and immediate contact between spectator and the neon. To compensate for the structural fragility of the neon, light intensities were stepped up to a point of nearly intolerable brilliance. The clear, fine linear definition, the maximized radiance and the inescapably ephemeral character of medium conspired to create a spectacular, nerve-tingling experience, which also required a certain mental agility on the spectator's part. The optical and structural fusion of form demanded a special alertness since perceptual dynamics were so powerfully present and distracting.

Chryssa has a talent for deliberately exposing and elucidating artistic process in her light box constructions. She is also an intelligent spokesman for her methods. She moves from rather prosaic if exact verbal description, so often involved in technology which requires elaborate explanation, to the statement of complex philosophic aims, with disarming digressions on the allure of her materials. Despite the 'found object' nature of her commercially fabricated transformed materials, Chryssa's journal sets forth the artistic aim of achieving a harmonious marriage of 'visions, material and technology'. Her perhaps simplistic remarks provide insight into the process by which mechanics, engineering and the material products of modern technology become mysteriously transformed into pure esthetic energy:

'The neon tubing shapes fragments of letters. The fragments I incorporate into my work are repeated like a machine product. The Plexiglas case that encloses the neon tubing repeats the work in all directions. To me this relates more to "measure" than reflection. Both sculpture and case relate to function. The shape gives light. It protects the fragile tubes and resembles night. The timer inserted in the lower section of the box measures time and functions in many different ways.

I choose the color of the case—Plexiglas Gray No. 2164—because it resembles night or darkness which relate to my original concept. All the words I have used mean something precise to me.

I FEEL STRONGLY ABOUT MEDIA AND MOST OF ALL ABOUT THE INDEPENDENCE OF MY LIGHT SCULPTURES FROM THEIR TECHNOLOGY. WHAT I MEAN IS THAT THE TRANSFORMERS WILL EVENTUALLY WEAR OUT.

Fortunately, there is the sun and the moon, day and night. Without electricity my sculpture will still survive.'

Significantly, Chryssa feels that the distinguishing feature of her works, their electrical illumination, is not an absolute or defining necessity, and urges that they be understood as a form of sculpture independent of the historical accident of contemporary technological existence.

'When the sculpture lights up,' she has remarked, 'it is only one aspect of "how it works." When the box is *not lit* it is the same thing . . . "how it works." For me it is like breathing, whether in or out.

The dark interval is never long enough for me. I do not expect or want anybody to wait for the moment when the sculpture lights up. I never do that myself when I have my works around me. I look THROUGH it all the time. That is how I communicate with these light or dark intervals.'

Discussing the dependence of Chryssa's work upon electricity for its full visual statement, a critic has characterized her work in this way: 'Each neon is like a science-fiction plant awaiting electricity to bloom.' Yet obviously for the artist the sculptural meaning of her work, although essentially defined and embodied by light, enjoys an independent existence in her own vivid and extremely concrete imagination. The individual work embodies such an intense and total reality for her that its cycle of blooming into light and momentary extinction into darkness are completely interconnected in the artist's mind. Such distinctions as the audience might necessarily make between the brilliant life of her illuminated, fragile neon tubes and the state of darkness when they no longer function do not hold any meaning for Chryssa. Her image's evocative power spans its illuminated and darkened phases, and each is resonantly implied by the other finally, in a kind of yin/yang relationship.

The alternately phantomic and solid material presence of her sculptural objects and Chryssa's conception of them seem connected to her ambivalent view of their absolute and relativistic character. Clearly, these mercurial sculptures in light at once embody and transcend their own time and technological condition. The artist tends to stress the universal content of her work despite its obvious and even acknowledged derivation from mass media sources.

In her journal she writes:

'The form of the sculpture should be separated from its surroundings natural or otherwise.

The nature and the technology of the material should not interfere with the sculpture itself. For instance, a light sculpture need not be lit, kinetic sculpture need not move.

If the value of the sculpture depends upon these elements then it becomes a gimmick. Also, it is the way the artist uses the material that matters and not the material itself that decides whether the sculpture is contemporary or not. When the artist expresses through the new material our time and thinking, he succeeds in creating a contemporary art object.'

In a period when the word 'major' has been devalued by the reckless extravagance of critical rhetoric, it is just as well to refrain from assessing for posterity the career of an artist who has only just turned forty. It does seem safe to hazard the opinion that Chryssa is one of the more significant woman artists of her generation. Even if her claim to fame rested only on one work, she would probably have a secure historical niche by reason of her magnificent *Gates to Times Square* (1964—66, page 55). This superlative achievement, a monumental, ten-foot-high construction in neon, steel, aluminum and Plexiglas, absorbed most of her energies over a two-year period, and still must rate as her most ambitious venture to date. The construction takes the form of an open three-dimensional triangle with a steeply sloping, roofed form supported by a monkey-puzzle grid of stainless steel divided by diagonal sheets of aluminum. These provide the framework for a honeycomb of stacked, vertical rows of massive metal letters interspersed with illuminated neon script, the latter housed in Plexiglas boxes. *The Gates* is decidedly architectural in scale and represents the *summa* of Chryssa's formal and imagistic preoccupations since she first began to work in neon. Many of her earlier motifs are, in fact, anthologized here in somewhat different form. Most impressively, the work reveals the inexhaustible variety of Chryssa's visual invention. With its environmental scale and varied presentation of light forms and material letters, it invites the spectator's interest and close examination, although the narrow, empty center is not designed to be negotiated by the viewer on foot. *The Gates* demonstrates a special synthesis of formal rigor, visual drama and elegance of statement which together are Chryssa's special expressive formula. She has managed to fuse an essentially constructivist idiom with contemporary fact, without in any way compromising the work's integrity or scintillating poetry of light.

The Gates proved a severe test of the artist's resourcefulness and persistence. When Chryssa experienced difficulty finding workmen or shop facilities for its fabrication, she proceeded to set up her own factory shop in a vacant industrial space, and there built most of the structure from scratch with her own hands and hired help. A professional glass blower provided the neon, and aluminum castings were made of the main structural elements. Her fierce artistic pride and refusal to be defeated by technical problems recalls David Smith's heroic individual efforts to be his own fabricator, and his symbolic act of identifying his studio in Bolton Landing by the industrial name of the Terminal Iron Works. Smith's artistic problems were, in fact, more susceptible to solution by individual exertion and handiwork, so long as there were chain hoists to move his heavy steel; in Chryssa's case, however, the intricacy of the new electric technology makes skilled help and an industrial plant virtually indispensable. When she was invited to stage a sizable one-man show at the Kassel *Documenta* in 1968, she was compelled to spend weeks searching through Holland and Germany for an appropriate industrial facility and knowledgeable technicians. She was finally successful in getting the requisite help, and then labored indefatigably for two months to produce a number of new works for her exhibition, including the monumental sixteen-foot-high, freestanding construction in neon, *Clytemnestra*. Her show was lavishly praised by European critics who found themselves sympathetic to work which combined the drama of heroic scale and the technological audacity which they associated with American art, and a refined, European sense of style—the same synthesis of artistic qualities which made *The Gates* such a spectacular achievement.

Something of the scope and intensity of this historic enterprise becomes clear from an illustrated, documentary journal which the artist compiled on *The Gates* in January of 1968, some four years after the vast project had been initiated. There she inventoried the specifications and described the background of the work, with an appropriate and cursory dryness, yet the more dramatic facts spoke for themselves:

'*The Gates*, 1964—66.

Welded stainless steel, neon and Plexiglas. Fragments of commercial signs also rolled plans for the forms. Also cast aluminum parts. 10 feet × 10 feet × 10 feet. *The Gates* took over two years to complete. I started by using original "commercial" signs. I then fitted these signs to the structure. Those "fragmented" commercial signs are enclosed in the Plexiglas boxes in the last two sections of *The Gates*. The last two sections focus on structure. Each of these fragments of the commercial signs is remade by me and repeated four times, in two or three places three times. I made 132 unrelated fragments and each section of the structure contains four, or three, depending on the position of the letters.'

Apropos of this description, and forming a convenient transition to Chryssa's esthetic principles, are some related remarks taken from a lecture delivered at New York University the same month she began to keep her notebook on *The Gates*. Here the idea of 'fragments' and the fragmentary is related to her sense of the discontinuities of contemporary experience. 'Since 1957', she declared in the written manuscript preserved from her lecture, 'I have worked in fragments. Entire areas of my newspaper paintings were covered with fragments of printed material. My "Gates" done eight years later are made with fragments of commercial signs as are my studies done in neon for the "Gates". I repeat these fragments, and in their entirety I reach reality. I cover the entire area with a fragment repeated precisely. There are slight variations in the fragments because a hand process is involved. This is the way my mind works, it has many intersections and impacts. Diagrams occur between the unconscious, instinctive directions.'

Some of the most revealing insights into Chryssa's artistic position were provided by her concluding remarks in the same lecture, which seems to contain the best general summary in her own words of the governing esthetic principles she follows. Of particular importance was the repeated insistence on artistic detachment, on retaining a 'cool mind', as she puts it, in the face of a virtual bombardment of information, visual sensation and conflicting esthetic viewpoints in the turbulent dynamism of American cultural life. Chryssa seems to take a particular delight in opening her sensibility to the currents and cross-currents of American life and art, but, as one may observe, she is also at pains to maintain her poise and objectivity lest she become a victim of shallow impressions:

'The roots of inspiration are continuously changing.

When I listen to the music of Bach I am aware of the "religious" element in his music but his genius DOMINATES this element and gives it a universal art value.

Today we establish our contemporary "Gods" and "Goddesses" in art, ephemeral, fragmentary and mechanical.

What I am trying to bring out here is the NEED to CONTROL our various roots of inspiration . . .

I think that the reality of the artist is the way he relates himself to both his sources of inspiration and the object he creates, and the way he controls them.

By approaching directly, physically—as is—the reality of the natural or the reality of the mechanical, or whatever is the root of inspiration from which our work springs, it seems to me that we do not reach the Real Reality in art . . .

I can only recall some of the ways my mind works:

Stage A:

Digging into one's self comes out to what may be a sincere and satisfying result but if it has already been done under another name it does not necessarily contribute anything to art.

Stage B:

The "tennis match" and "why pigeons fly" * is closer to THE WAY, a self-condition that is hard to nail down but which I can best describe as a "cool mind". This is the stage when the mind "works" in the area of the impersonal and which to me is very close to the realization of the universal self.'

Here Chryssa refers for the second time to the 'cool mind', and to its ability to absorb contemporary information and raw experience without being overwhelmed, or losing sight of its own artistic reality:

'I mean several things when I say the "cool mind". For example:

A mind that is already charged with "storage" information.

A mind that is avoiding its own pattern of thinking; discoveries of yesterday should not become the Mannerisms of tomorrow. A new logic should be found. Times Square, an area that offered me, in the last ten years, several stimulants of the mind, no longer relates to me in the same way. Its reality is no longer a part of my reality. I am trying to resolve a "way of working out values" which I cannot reach only through logic or instincts, or courage, or storage. When my endless monologues with sculpture become too familiar to me, too much a part of me, then I usually abandon them because when they reach that stage they no longer work out.

And I also feel that the "cool mind" is a mind that never gives up the endless struggle of "working out new logics".

A mind willing to experiment, to "go through" this storage information and yet to keep its freedom. A mind that always takes over, and refuses to be "controlled".

A mind that starts new all the time, keeps "feeding" and "storing" all the time, exercises all the time.

* These comparisons and zen-like aphorisms of artistic activities, in the realm of physical phenomena, allude to earlier portions of the artist's lecture.

A mind that goes beyond the limits of technology and of the material and is independent of both.

A mind that is free as much as possible from unconscious automatism of every sort or unconscious overt drives of every sort, sadistic, masochistic, etc.

A mind that is aware of psycho-aesthetic make-ups, optical illusions based on certain geometric arrangements or color relations, etc.

A mind that deals with areas of TODAY and expresses our contemporary way of thinking and seeing . . .

A mind that is aware of its own reality.'

Thus, Chryssa represents to herself, with considerable confidence and clarity, her own process of thought in the abstract, while she at the same time acknowledges the truths of technological reality, and her own temperamental bias. The results promote both fresh invention and creativity, and her conception of the 'cool mind' reveals the surprising contemporary outlines of a new classicism, in which we recognize familiar attributes of clarity, order and intellectual control.

Chryssa's recent work has been among her most extraordinary, simultaneously renewing familiar themes and testing new grounds. One of the most brilliant and satisfying of her light boxes is *Automat* (1971, page 68), a slim, five-foot-high, dark Plexiglas box, not quite two feet wide, which houses letters well known to all New York streetgoers who have ever eaten at the ubiquitous Horn and Hardart's self-service cafeterias. The word 'Automat' is spelled out twice in banks of half-letters which are completed by their echoing lateral reflections in the dark but lustrous glass, glimmering like a suspended illusionistic mirage. The two rows of half-letters also complete each other vertically like their own reflections. The end views through the glass box are perhaps most astonishing of all in their ruby-red, brilliant dazzle and baroque confusion of overlaid letters, a latter-day celtic interlace in neon, formally related to the earlier *Analysis of Letter B* (1963, page 51). For ecstatic, burning luminosity, and formal complication and resolution, the ensemble is simply unsurpassed in her entire *œuvre*. Like so much of Chryssa's work, a simple and coherent scheme is made just sufficiently intricate to give one a satisfying sense of richness without suggesting a too involved demonstration of problem solving. The alterations in letter positions and in the angles of vision, and the interplay of letters and reflections which complete the tangible neon forms recall Jasper Johns once again. Chryssa and Johns share an interest in lettered forms and common signs, and both artists use the esthetic potential of such forms both for expressive ambiguity and crystalline clarity. Yet the intellectual content of the work, with its varied modes of representation, would only be hollow without Chryssa's mysteriously effective ability to achieve sensuous beauty. Indeed, it is the luminous intensity of the work, veiled by the dark Plexiglas, which hints at the potential of passion when the controlling rheostat is adjusted to its highest pitch of brilliance.

The automat theme evolved interestingly from ensembles of accidentally positioned plaster letters in shallow relief, combined with sparse neon elements, as in the smaller *Automat* model (in the collection of the Harry N. Abrams Family). With these preliminary studies, Chryssa returned to the inspiration of her early *Bach* boxes, and their multiple views of letters spelling out a word, the ancient method of Cubist simultaneity scrupulously reinterpreted in a three-dimensional constructivist form. By doubling up and symmetrizing her letter forms, Chryssa created a more self-contained formal structure. In the *Automat* study, however, the random scatter of some letters dispersed the regimented columns and rows of other white plaster letters, creating an effect of studied carelessness. She used neon with virtuoso skill, selectively repeating the opaque block letters in refulgent colored light.

The relief *N's*, of the same period, betrays a more orderly arrangement of the letter theme. The uniformly repeated letter N creates regularized, parallel horizontal and vertical rows which nonetheless generate considerable optical ambiguity and energies. Their implied vector-like movement into their ground recalls the directional thrust of the explicit arrow forms of Chryssa's earliest work. This, then, is another instance of a retrospective idea which gains fresh impetus and renewed formal power in a new context. The neon letter 'N' at the center of the latticework composition provides another kind of variety in representation, and coloristic relief from the chalky white monochrome.

It is worth noting that these recent constructions were carried out at a rather desperate time like so many others throughout her rather precarious career, when Chryssa was hard-up, short of funds and quite literally unable to finance the expensive, elaborate technology her art demanded. If neon is thus not an emphatic note in these works, and her materials are otherwise necessarily modest—befitting the rather chaste formal decor of her constructions—then the economic bases for these austere choices, and their possible expressive limitation, were immediately turned to her esthetic advantage.

Chryssa's sense of rationalizing, flattening, and deliberately sorting out her imagery and lettered signs, rather like a Mercator projection of the world, gives intelligibility, coherence and an almost classical sense of order even to her most emotional, electrified sculpture. This is not to say that Chryssa's work does not derive from emotional experience, or carry its impress in the final, resolved image. A case in point is *Clytemnestra,* which the artist subtitled 'The first scream from Iphigenia in Aulis by Euripides'. When the work was first shown in a New York gallery in 1967, the artist discussed its genesis with a reporter, who observed to her that the orifice of blue-black tubing could be compared to a visualized scream. Chryssa responded with the information that the work was, in fact, inspired by the Greek actress Irene Pappas, who at the time was playing the role of Clytemnestra in a production in the Village directed by the artist's friend, Michael Cacoyannis. Chryssa is reported to have then said: 'When Clytemnestra first learns that Agamemnon intends to sacrifice their daughter Iphigenia, Pappas twists her body into a shocked S and screams. That is what I am trying to show with this neon.' However, she has also indicated in her notes that the work was part of the continuing series of studies for *The Gates to Times Square*, proving in the same reporter's words that 'classic myth and papaya juice stands are not mutually exclusive'. Of course, what Chryssa demonstrated was that a profound emotional inspiration and a modern structural esthetic can coexist, and harmoniously interact. She also proved once again that the most banal imagery and commonplace ciphers of the contemporary world, and the technology which breeds them in ever new forms, can be adapted to the universal values of a rigorous, modern abstract art.

Curiously, other artists in Europe and America who worked in neon have almost without exception been limited by the popular character of their art, and soon exhausted formal invention when the impact of their imagery palled. Since Chryssa's letter variations are essentially abstract ciphers despite their obvious connotative meanings, and are governed by a complex artistic evolution, her work continues to nourish itself on the same sources which sustain the vital non-objective art of our time.

Today, one can applaud in particular her courage as an artist of inventive capacity willing to undertake ambitious ventures; her finest moment was probably *The Gates to Times Square*, one of the truly impressive sculptures of the American post-war period—and a work surely that belongs in a museum, where it would be accessible to young artists and take its place in the evolutionary order of contemporary sculpture. Her recent attempts at mural, billboard scale in *Boogie Woogie* and other exhibited studies for even more monumental, perhaps for the moment only visionary constructions, seem to indicate that Chryssa's ambition and willingness to take risks remain undiminished. At forty years of age, at the peak of her creative powers, and once again working productively with the kind of intensity and concentration that have produced her finest shows, Chryssa may be the only 'light' artist in America who has managed to transcend the limitations of working with pop imagery and the facile, technical seductions of her chosen neon medium.

However, she herself tends to take a less encouraging view of her recent triumphs. 'All those pieces,' she complained recently, 'have been for me a disaster, financially and in every way. When I do work on a large scale, I must invest everything I have materially, and my entire existence, my health, in my work. I live by the most inhuman schedule . . . I sleep in my clothes.' Like many contemporary sculptors, but perhaps even more so than most, she finds that the materials, technology, and special fabrication her work entails are extremely costly. Even her moderate-size light boxes require expenditures of thousands of dollars. Nor is there any assurance that the large works of the past, such as *The Gates*, or her newer ventures on a comparable scale will find a willing purchaser at the sometimes stunning prices she now feels compelled to ask, which in turn reflect her astronomical manufacturing costs. Until very recently she had no dealer and was forced to subsidize her own work; staggering factory bills accumulated at an alarming rate. While she is not indigent, and collectors and museums continue to seek out her new work in her studio, one does get the impression that her normal state of anxiety and creative tension have more validity now than usual. But one also entertains the suspicion that Chryssa generates crises purposely, if unconsciously, to provide a motive for then dispelling them—through the catharsis of work. For most of us, such an habitual state of emergency would be too hard on the nerves to be long endured. Chryssa, however, seems to thrive in a high-risk environment, and her best work flows out of a continuing sense of drama and crisis.

Not very long ago, she received a visitor in her crowded, narrow floor-through apartment-cum-studio on the upper East Side. The apartment serves both as living and working space, small and cramped though it is. The larger mechanical constructions are fabricated elsewhere, of course. As she spoke about her work, her expressive, sunshine-and-showers face momentarily screwed itself into a frown: her landlord was threatening eviction, since her lease was nearly up—an old story! She needed all her wits and powers of concentration to complete the newest group of sculptures, which would be magnificent, but life was an unending series of costly, taxing interruptions—the latest took the form at that instant of crated work arriving from an exhibition just terminated. In the meantime, there was the distraction of the phone, ringing unendingly. Her austere living room, which consists mainly of a couple of couches, chairs and a large ten-foot-square table under a Noguchi paper lantern, piled high with unopened letters, drawings, albums of installation photographs, jammed ash trays (for she smokes incessantly), discarded clothes and remnants of distant meals, was an indescribable mess. The disorder, one was assured, represented only a momentary aberration, and would be dealt with briskly just as soon as she was released by the demon of work, the relentless demands of the phone, and permitted to 'breathe again'. However harassed Chryssa may appear to be, besieged though she is by the hostile forces of urban life which include landlords, deadlines, unfinished projects, logistical problems and other distractions, the continuity of her work and her immense productivity do seem to remain miraculously unaffected.

She is fortunate in having a few loyal and genuinely concerned friends, who range from anonymous Greek countrymen living quiet, private lives in New York to the affluent and powerful of this world. They do what they can to make her American existence more bearable, but it is unlikely they will succeed in significantly calming her anxieties, or appeasing her *Wanderlust*. Like many artists, her preferred condition is nomadic. She resembles her work in that she can never quite decide to come to rest, or to accept any simple or obvious solution, like staying rooted in one locale for an unbroken period of time. 'For the creative person', she solemnly declares in her most becoming sibylline manner, 'life is like a play—you continue until you reach your destiny'.

Cycladic Book, 1955

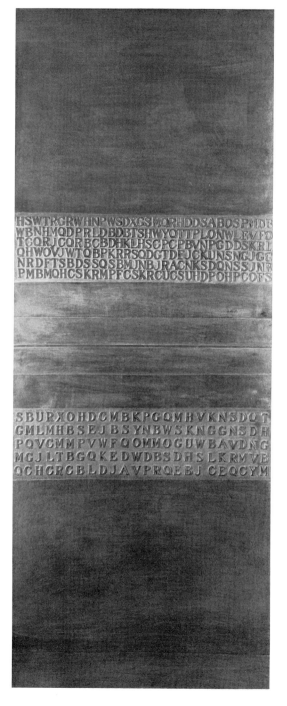

◁ Arrow Homage to Times Square, 1957

Letter E, 1957—60

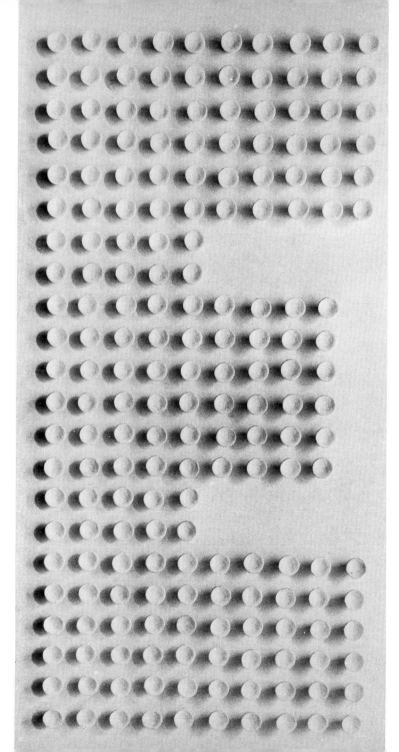

Letter H, 1957–60

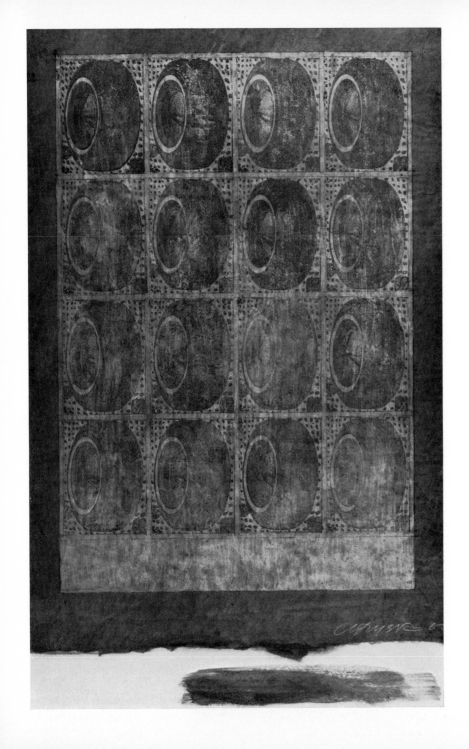

Cigarette Lighter, 1959—62

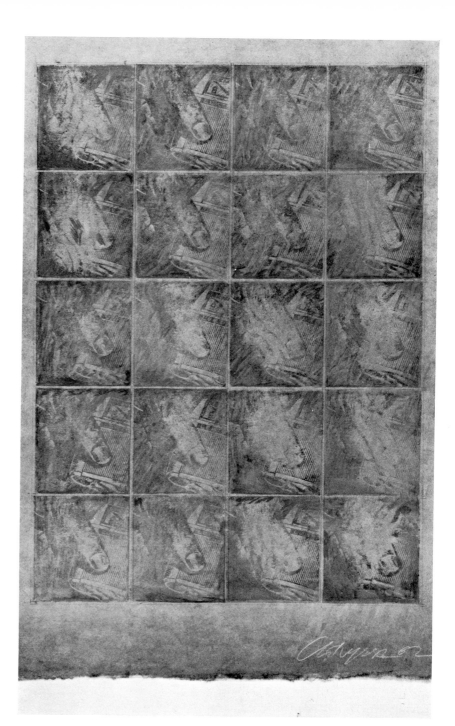

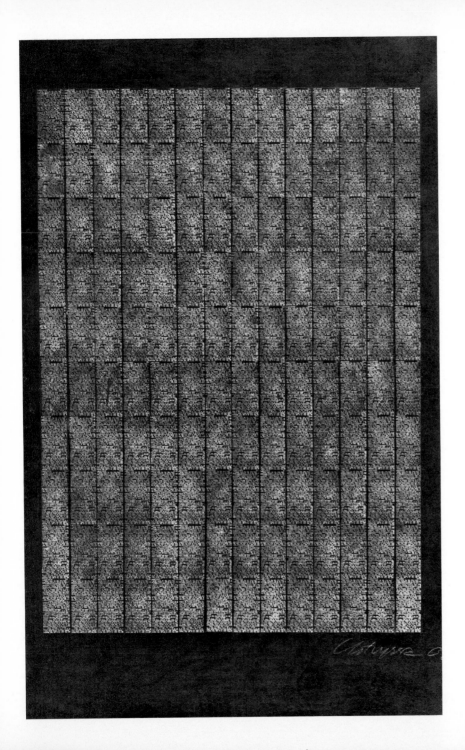

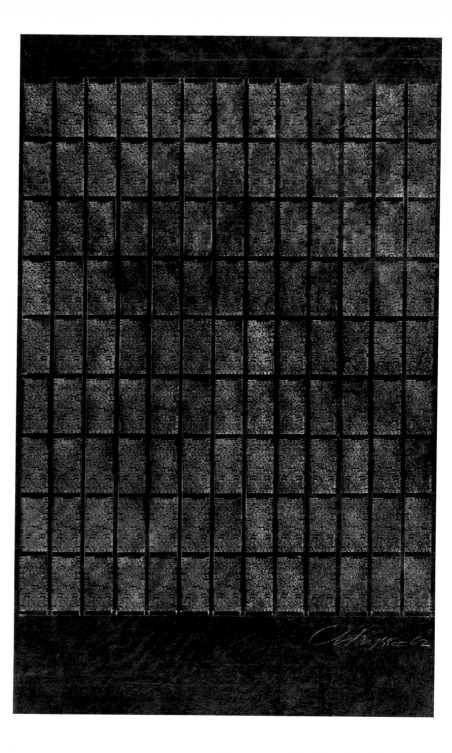

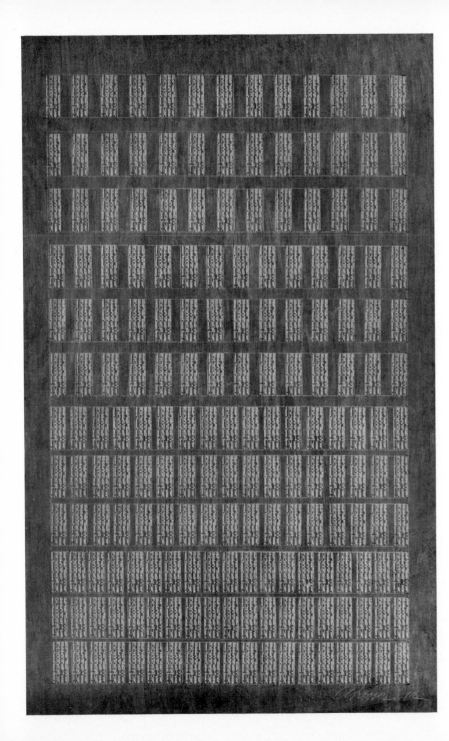

Stocks, 1959—62

Times Square Puzzle, 1962 ▷

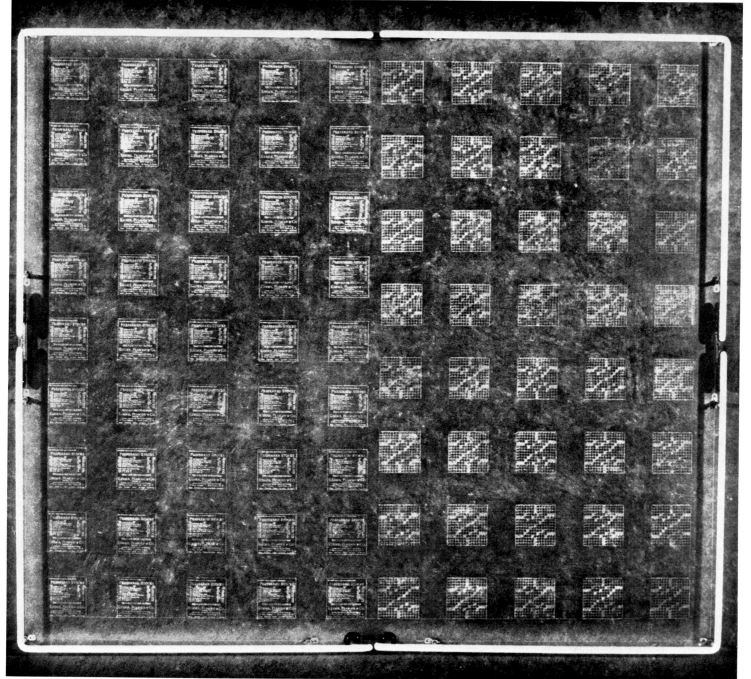

Guitar, 1960

◁　Times Square Sky (Air), 1961–62

Americanoom, 1963

43

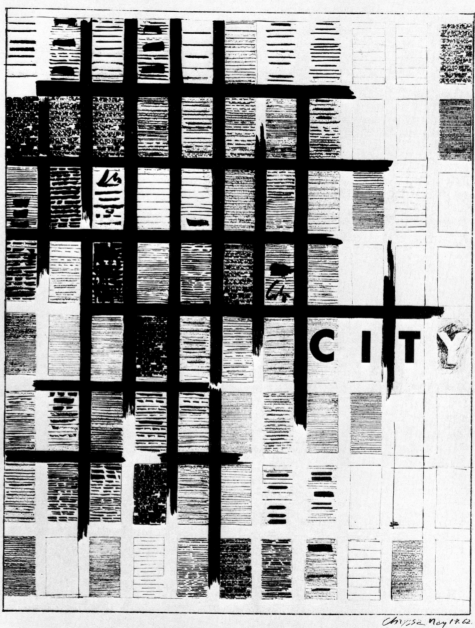

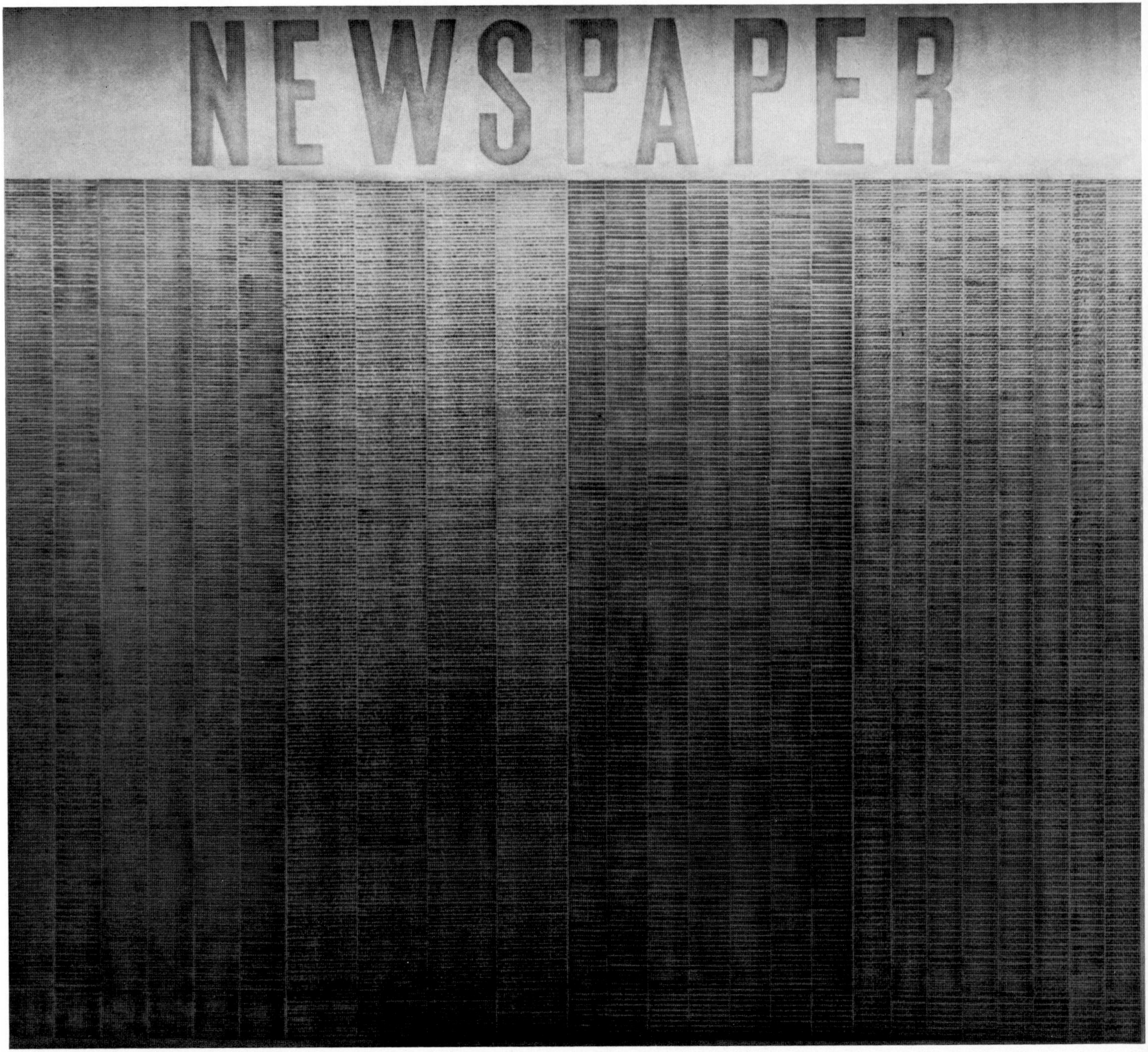
NEWSPAPER

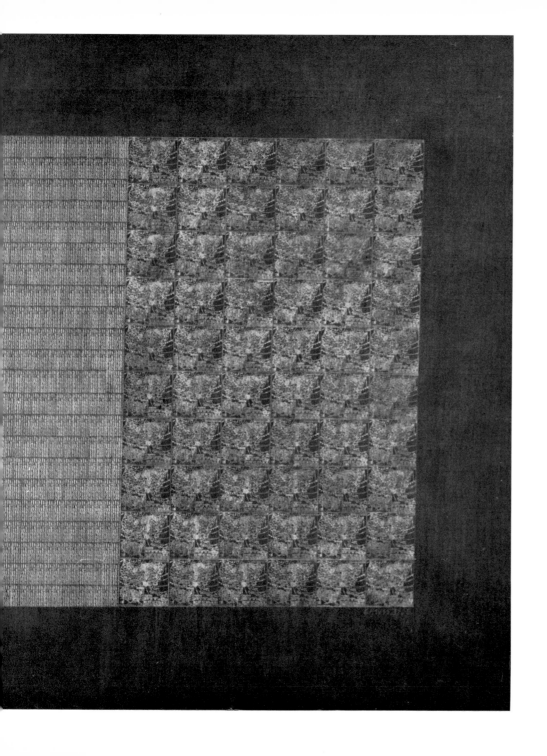

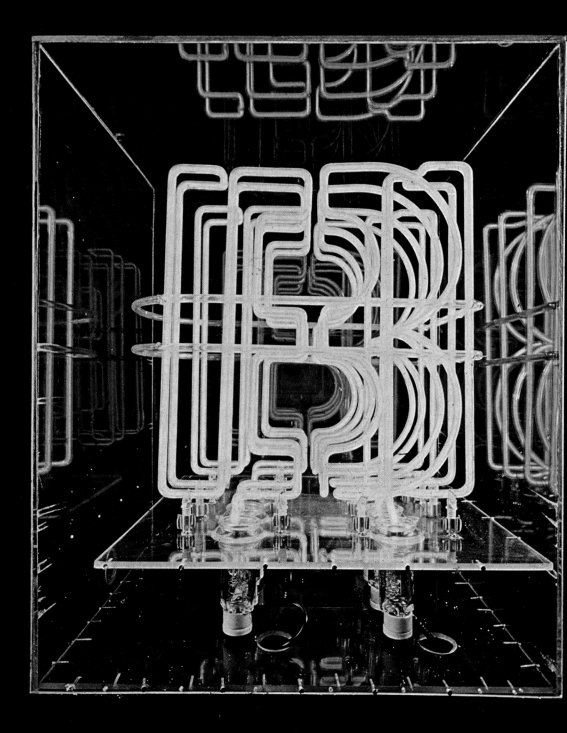

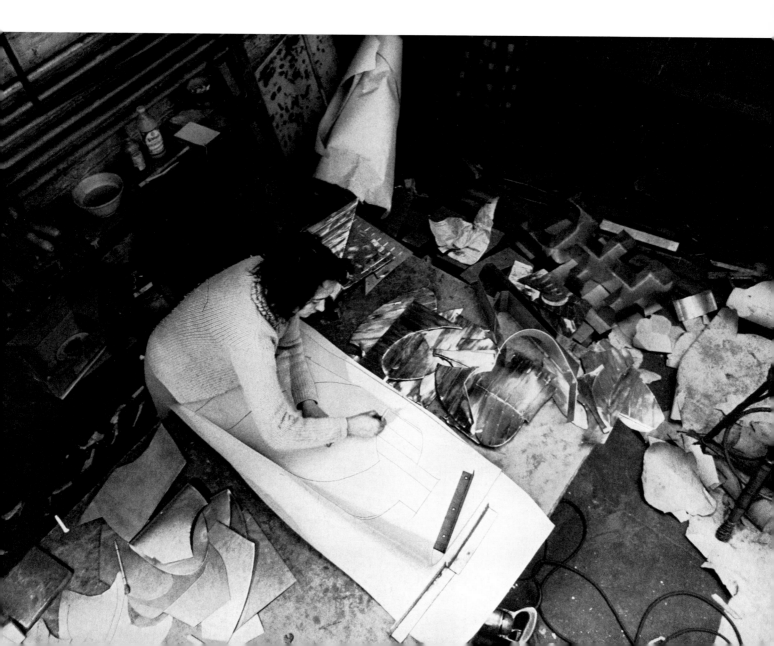

Delicatessen, 1965

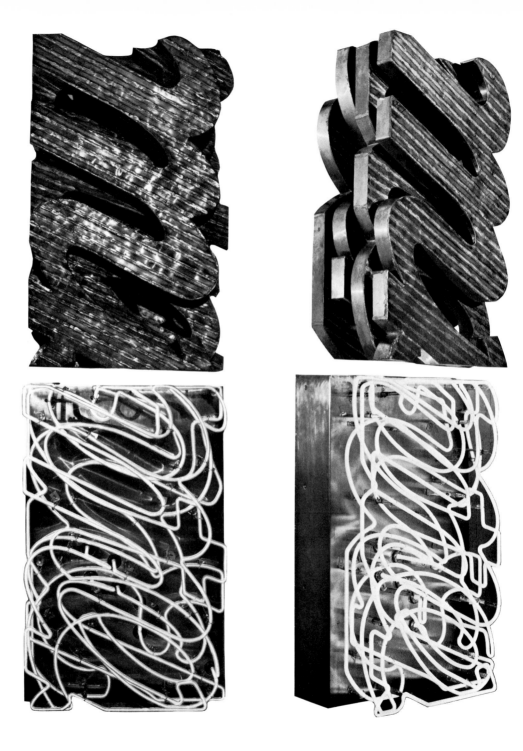

Study for the Gates, No. 15 (Flock of Morning Birds from Iphigenia in Aulis by Euripides), 1967

Clytemnestra No. 1 (The First Scream from Iphigenia in Aulis by Euripides), 1966

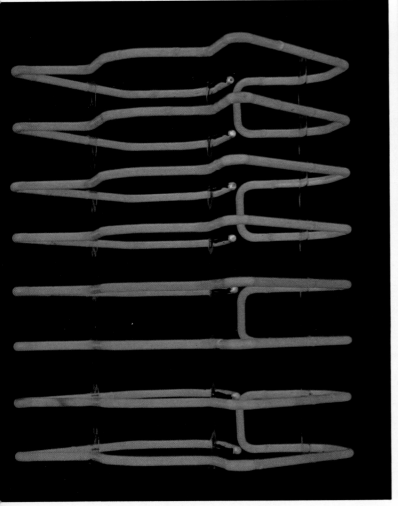

Study for the Gates, No. 3,
1966—67

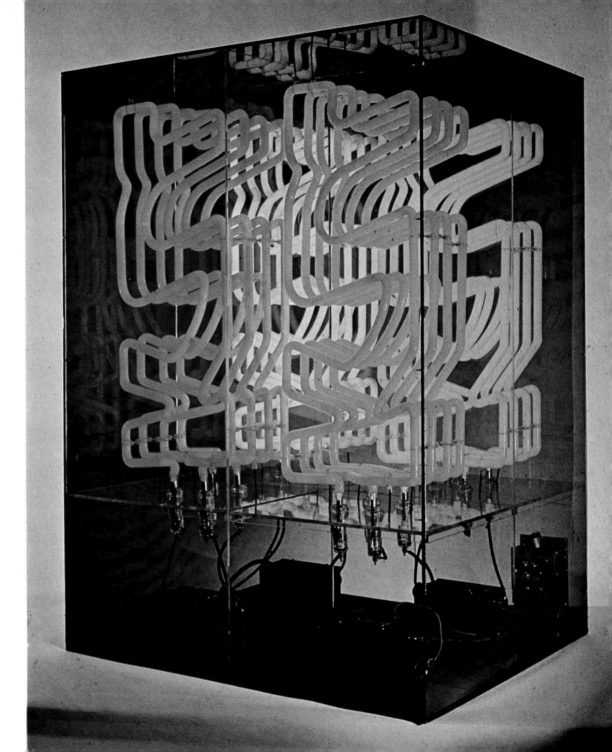

◁ Study for the Gates, No. 5, 1967

Study for the Gates, No. 4, 1967

Clytemnestra, 1968
(Nationalgalerie, Berlin)

65

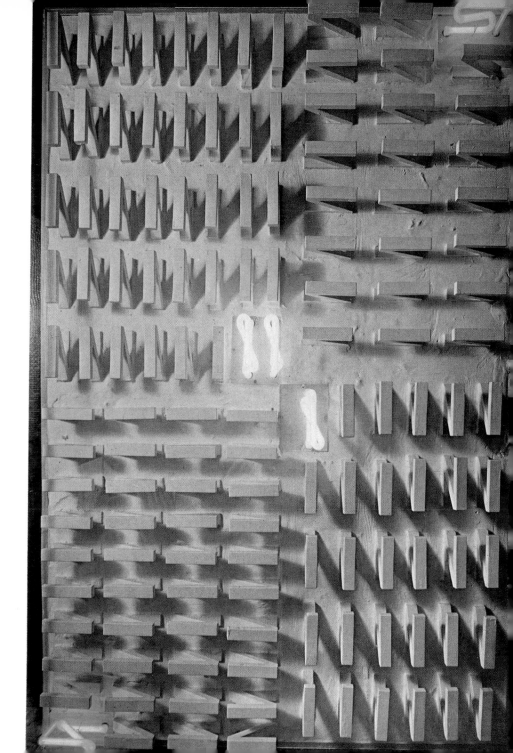

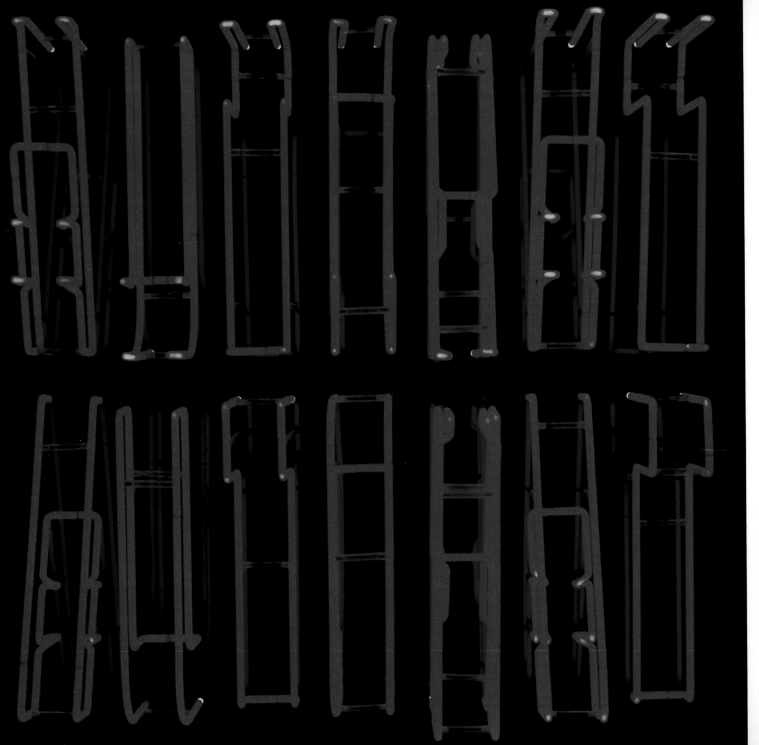

Birds, 1969

Cents Sign
Travelling from Broadway
to Africa via Guadeloupe
1968   ▷

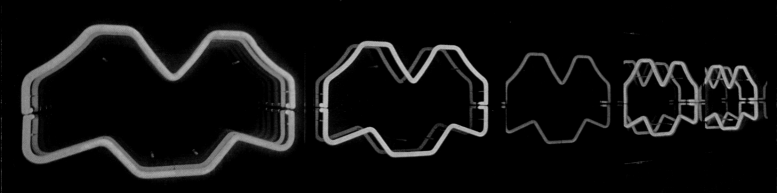

(24 × 24 × 15″). Collection Mr. and Mrs. Horace H. Solomon, New York

52–53 Pencil sketches for *The Gates to Times Square*

54 The artist with metal forms for *The Gates to Times Square*

55 *The Gates to Times Square*, 1964–66
Welded stainless steel, neon tubing, Plexiglas, fragments of commercial signs, rolled plans for the forms, and cast aluminum, 3,05 × 3,05 × 3,05 m (120 × 120 × 120″). Albright-Knox Art Gallery, Buffalo. Gift of Mr. and Mrs. Albert A. List

56 *Ampersand No. 4*, 1964
Multicolored neon tubing, edition of three, 0,77 × 0,35 × 0,28 m (30 $^1/_4$ × 13 $^3/_4$ × 11 $^1/_8$″). The work consists of five approaches to the subject of the Ampersand. The Museum of Modern Art, New York; Harry N. Abrams Family Collection, New York; Private collection

57 *Ampersand No. 3*, 1964
Multicolored neon tubing, edition of three, 0,77 × 0,35 × 0,28 m (30 $^1/_4$ × 13 $^3/_4$ × 11 $^1/_8$″). The work consists of five approaches to the subject of the Ampersand. The Museum of Modern Art, New York; Harry N. Abrams Family Collection, New York; Private collection

58 *Delicatessen*, 1965
Welded stainless steel and Plexiglas, 2,08 × 0,50 × 0,38 m (82 × 19 $^1/_2$ × 15″). Collection Mr. and Mrs. Albert A. List, New York

59 *Positive/Negative*, 1965–66
Stainless steel and neon tubing, 1,65 × 0,52 × 0,29 m (65 × 20 $^1/_2$ × 11 $^1/_2$″). Collection Mr. and Mrs. Max Wasserman, Boston

60 At left:
Study for the Gates, No. 15 (Flock of Morning Birds from "Iphigenia in Aulis" by Euripides), 1967
Neon tubing with timer, 1,57 × 0,90 × 0,75 m (62 × 35 $^1/_2$ × 29 $^3/_8$″). The Hirshhorn Museum and Sculpture Garden, Smithsonian Institution, Washington, D.C.
At right:
Clytemnestra No. 1 (The First Scream from "Iphigenia in Aulis" by Euripides), 1966
Neon tubing and rheostat, 1,30 × 1,00 × 0,72 m (51 × 39 $^1/_2$ × 29″). Corcoran Gallery of Art, Washington, D.C.

61 *Study for the Gates, No. 3*, 1966–67
Neon tubing and Plexiglas with timer, 1,19 × 0,90 × 0,72 m (47 × 35 $^1/_2$ × 28 $^1/_2$″). Collection Franzen Rick, New York

62 *Study for the Gates, No. 5*, 1967
Neon tubing and Plexiglas with timer, 1,09 × 0,88 × 0,70 m (43 × 34 $^1/_2$ × 27 $^1/_2$″). Collection the artist

63 *Study for the Gates, No. 4*, 1967
Neon tubing and Plexiglas with timer, 1,09 × 0,88 × 0,70 m (43 × 34 $^1/_2$ × 27 $^1/_2$″). Tate Gallery, London

64–65 *Clytemnestra*, 1968
Multicolored neon tubing and molded Plexiglas with timer, 4,88 × 2,74 m (192 × 108″). Page 64 as installed at the "4. Documenta," Kassel, Germany, 1968; page 65 as installed at the Nationalgalerie, Berlin

66 *N's*, 1970
Pencil, 1,17 × 0,76 m (46 × 30″). Collection Mrs. Helen W. Benjamin, New York

67 *N's*, 1970
Plaster, neon tubing and Plexiglas, 1,17 × 0,78 × 0,23 m (46 × 31 × 9″). Collection Mrs. Litsa Tsitsera, New York

68 *Automat*, 1971
Neon tubing, bronze-colored Plexiglas, and rheostat, 1,73 × 1,73 × 0,51 m (68 × 68 × 20″). Harry N. Abrams Family Collection, New York

69 *Times Square Sign*, 1970–73
Asbestos, painted aluminum, and Plexiglas, 2,44 × 2,74 m (96 × 108″). Collection the artist

70 *Birds*, 1969
Neon tubing and Plexiglas, edition of three, 1,19 × 1,42 × 0,27 m (47 × 56 × 10 $^1/_2$″). Galerie Der Spiegel, Cologne; Jean Larcade, Paris; Collection the artist

71 *Cents Sign Travelling from Broadway to Africa via Guadeloupe*, 1968
Neon tubing, colored metal, silkscreen, and Plexiglas, c. 1,98 × 1,09 × 0,74 m (78 × 43 × 29″). Collection the artist

72 The artist in her Brooklyn workshop

One-man Exhibitions

1961   Betty Parsons Gallery, New York
        The Solomon R. Guggenheim Museum, New York
1962   Cordier & Ekstrom, New York
1963   The Museum of Modern Art, New York
1965   Institute of Contemporary Art, University of Pennsylvania, Philadelphia
1966   Pace Gallery, New York
1968   Pace Gallery, New York
        Harvard University, Dept. of Fine Arts, Cambridge, Mass.
        Walker Art Center, Minneapolis
        Galerie Rive Droite, Paris
1969   Obelisk Gallery, Boston
        Galerie Der Spiegel, Cologne
1970   Graphics Gallery, San Francisco
        Galleria d'Arte Contemporanea, Torino, Italy
1972   Whitney Museum of American Art, New York
1973   Galerie Denise René, New York

Selected Group Exhibitions

1960   Whitney Museum of American Art, New York: "Annual Exhibition of Contemporary American Drawings and Sculpture"
        Martha Jackson Gallery, New York: "New Forms, New Media"
1960–61   The Museum of Modern Art, New York: "Recent Acquisitions"
1961   Boston Arts Festival
        Galerie Rive Droite, Paris: "Le Nouveau Réalisme"
        Carnegie Institute, Museum of Art, Pittsburgh: "The 42nd Pittsburgh International Exhibition of Contemporary Painting and Sculpture"
1962   Whitney Museum of American Art, New York: "Annual Exhibition of Contemporary American Drawings and Sculpture"
1963   Tour Exhibition organized by the American Federation of Arts: "New Directions"
        Seattle World's Fair, Arts Pavilion
        VII Bienal de São Paulo, U.S. Section, organized by the Walker Art Center, Minneapolis: "Ten American Sculptors" (1964: Walker Art Center, Minneapolis; San Francisco Museum of Art; City Art Museum of St. Louis; The Dayton Art Institute, Dayton, Ohio; Howard Wise Gallery, New York)
        The Museum of Modern Art, New York: "Americans 1963"
1964   Instituto Torcuato Di Tella, Museo de Artes Visuales, Buenos Aires
        Carnegie Institute, Museum of Art, Pittsburgh: "The 1964 Pittsburgh International Exhibition of Contemporary Painting and Sculpure"
        The Museum of Modern Art, New York: "Prints of Sculptors and Painters"
        New School for Social Research, New York: "International Sculpture Show"
        Arts Council, Philadelphia: "Dial for Sculpture"
        Rose Art Museum, Brandeis University, Waltham, Mass.: "New Directions in American Painting and Sculpture"
1965   Pace Gallery, New York: "Beyond Realism"
1966   Stedelijk van Abbemuseum, Eindhoven: "Kunst Licht Kunst"

Whitney Museum of American Art, New York: "Art of the United States 1670—1966"
Finch College Museum of Art, New York: "Art in Process"
The Jewish Museum, New York: "The Harry N. Abrams Family Collection"
The Museum of Modern Art, New York: "Contemporary Painters and Sculptors as Printmakers"
The Art Institute of Chicago: "68th American Exhibition"
Institute of Contemporary Art, Boston: "Multiplicity"
1966—67 Whitney Museum of American Art, New York: "1966 Annual Exhibition: Sculpture and Prints"
1967 Walker Art Center, Minneapolis: "Light — Motion — Space"
New Jersey State Museum, Trenton: "Focus on Light"
Yale University Art Gallery, New Haven: "The Helen W. and Robert M. Benjamin Collection"
The Museum of Modern Art, New York: "Art of the Sixties"
Los Angeles County Museum of Art; Philadelphia Museum of Art: "American Sculpture of the Sixties"
New York City Festival: "Sculpture in Environment"
Worcester Art Museum, Worcester, Mass.: "Light and Motion"
Sidney Janis Gallery, New York: "Exhibition of Work by Leading Artists in Homage to Marilyn Monroe"
1968 Kassel, Germany: "4. Documenta"
1970—71 Whitney Museum of American Art, New York: "1970 Annual Exhibition: Contemporary American Sculpture"
1972 XXXVI Mostra Biennale Internazionale d'Arte, Venice